GROWING PAINS

BY TOM GILL

Published by Playdead Press 2018

© Tom Gill 2018

Tom Gill has asserted his rights under the Copyright, Design and Patents Act, 1988, to be identified as the author of this work.

A CIP catalogue record for this book is available from the British Library.

ISBN 978-1-910067-63-5

Caution
All rights whatsoever in this play are strictly reserved and application for performance should be sought through the author before rehearsals begin. No performance may be given unless a license has been obtained.

This book is sold subject to the condition that it shall not by way of trade or otherwise, be lent, resold, hired out, or otherwise circulated without the publisher's prior consent in any form of binding or cover other than that in which it is published and without a similar condition including this condition being imposed on the subsequent purchaser.

Playdead Press
www.playdeadpress.com

TOM GILL | Writer/Performer

Tom is an award winning actor, spoken word artist, and singer/songwriter from Salford. He is a UK National Poetry Slam Champion, and a former resident artist at the Roundhouse in Camden.

He was winner of the Lyrical Firewards Award in association with Paines Plough, and has featured at an eclectic mix of venues and festivals from Ronnie Scott's Jazz Club to Latitude, Wilderness and Lovebox festival.

Tom has had work commissioned and televised by Channel 4 and Sky One, as well as collaborating on projects with BBC Radio 1Xtra and Manchester United/Adidas.

GROWING PAINS was originally commissioned by Battersea Arts Centre, and premiered at the Underbelly as part of Edinburgh Fringe Festival 2016.

As an actor Tom's theatre credits include *FIRST LIGHT* (Chichester festival Theatre); *BUCKETS* (Orange Tree Theatre); *LINES* (The Yard Theatre); *GOODBYE BARCELONA* (Arcola Theatre); *DUNSINANE* (National Theatre of Scotland/RSC).

His film credits include *PETERLOO* (Dir. Mike Leigh); *DUNKIRK* (Dir. Christopher Nolan) and *EDEN LAKE* (Dir. James Watkins).

The Growing Pains EP Album is available to download. Go to www.tom-gill.co.uk

MATTHEW LANDERS | Director/Dramaturg

Matthew is a director, screen writer, playwright and poet from the northwest of England.

After winning the 2005 John Hartley award for poetry Matthew's first play '*Arrows*' was winner of the Willy Russell Foundation Award for best new script. His next '*A Dog Called Redemption*' won the Manchester Evening News award for best new play and the Oscar Wilde Award for excellence at the Dublin Theatre festival.

In 2015 he was commissioned to write the first episode of his TV thriller '*Innocent*' by Big Talk Productions. '*Twockers*' is in development with Blue Bear Productions and his comedy drama '*Rusholme Raj*' has been optioned by Hat Trick Productions. Matthew was also co-writer of '*Prospects*' a drama/reality project for Avalon

Matthew is an associate of the Listeners project; an artistic collective who create short films and poems. He has also worked as a teacher/educator in Dramatic art and the English language in some of the most deprived areas in the country.

EWAN PHILLIPS | Music/Sound Production

Ewan is a producer, composer and multi skilled musician. He studied at The University of Manchester where he won the H.P Leonard Prize for composition and has since been acting as a studio engineer/producer for a number of up and coming artists. He is founder of production company HigherSound.

Growing Pains is supported by house Theatre.

house supports venues by improving the range, quality and scale of theatre presented across South East and Eastern England, and exists to build the audience for contemporary theatre across the region.

house is delivered by Farnham Maltings, and steered by a group of regional programmers and producers comprising Brighton Dome, Colchester Arts Centre, Corn Exchange Newbury, Harlow Playhouse, New Wolsey Theatre Ipswich, Oxford Playhouse, South Street Reading, and The Point Eastleigh.

house is supported by Arts Council England.

DIRECTORS NOTE

The process behind Growing Pains was an exciting and unusual one. Tom approached me explaining he wanted to fashion some of his work into a one man show. From the outset we both wanted to do something other than a simple anthology of his work, stitched together with a loose theme that was the trend for spoken word shows at the time. Tom's other skills as an actor and musician were something I desperately wanted to utilize to create a piece that was a mixture of music, theatre, comedy as well as poetry. A show with characters, songs and scenes punctuating the verse to heighten its power and draw the audience in. We worked on Tom's old work at first trying to shoe horn it into a story but found that the more we workshopped ideas the more we realised that original verse written specifically for the developing show was needed to drive the story. Tom rose to the challenge linking all the brand new songs, scenes and characters together with blistering verse and embodying every character on the stage through countless hours of character work in the rehearsal room. The result was Growing Pains a poetic play come musical come state of the nation piece that I'm immensely proud of being a part of. I hope this book allows it another life beyond our influence.

Matthew Landers

A massive thanks to Norman and May Bottomley for their continued support. A special thanks to Matthew Landers for his hard work and dedication, and to all those who've supported the production along the way.

Growing Pains
By Tom Gill

Characters

TOM
GIRL IN PARK
HOWARD.
ROB.
LEE.
NICK.
SAV.
CHEEKY.
MUM.
DAD.
KAREN
CHARLIE.
BETH.
BART

Note on Text.

Spoken Word/Dialogue in Regular

Songs in *Bold Italics*

Stage Directions/Action in Italics

Sirens.

TOM.   And all I can see is his eyes. But it's not his
eyes I'm seeing.
I'm not seeing his eyes; I'm seeing *his* eyes.
And I want to stick a knife in them.
I want to steal the life from them.
I want those eyes red
I want those eyes bled
I want those eyes dead.
I can hear Beth scream. I can hear her
stream of tears
But this is years...
There's spilt beer
But it's not here.
None of it's here
It's just me and him.
It's just me.
And *him.*

Sirens. Screams. Door slams.

Part 1. Salford.

TOM.   So I slam the front door shut,
Tell them they're a bunch of knobs,
And make my way out of the estate,
To my best mate Rob's.

Now everyone just buzzes off Rob coz he's
got dreadlocks,
But I buzz off Rob, cuz I think that he's
dead top!
And his family are mint.
A proper mad combination.
His mum's really short and from Bolton.
His dad's really tall, and he's Jamaican!

9

And as I'm making my way to his house,
Carrying the weight of the world in my J.D
sports bag
That's strapped to my back,
To replace my rucksack,
That was slashed by some lad,
Wearing the badge
'Cock of Year 10' on his fat fod,
Like he's some sort of God,
I'm feeling proper pissed off.

I pass these two girls I recognize from the
year above,
Who are stood in some counterfeit pose,
Wearing what looks like pajamas
But apparently they're clothes,
And as I get close,
I hear the polyphonic tones of my Motorola
phone
And it's playing Boys 2 Men as I-

(Singing)

'Come, to the end of the rooooaaad...'

I'm well embarrassed,
So I quickly try and stop it.
Dive into my bag to find this shit brick
That I couldn't even fit in my fucking
pocket.

One of 'em gets cocky, tries to belittle,
Says,

GIRL IN PARK. Eyyarr, did you know that you're little?

TOM.　　　But little, did I know,
That call would change my entire mood see,

10

Cuz I've just found out I'm gonna be in a movie!

So now I'm bouncing down these streets
Feeling empowered.
And as I reach the end of Robs drive,
In the garden, I see his dad

Howard.

HOWARD.   Robert? ROBERT? Ya friends here! Alright Tom. Robert tells me you're gonna be a famous actor someday boy?

TOM.   Yeah, well that's the plan Howard.

HOWARD.   Y'got any roles comin' up?

TOM.   Y'what mate?

HOWARD.   You got any roles coming up? Roles? Roles?

TOM.   Oh roles, you mean like parts? Yeah, well funny you should ask actually Howard, cuz I just got a call on the way here, to say I've got a part in this new film.

HOWARD.   Ah that's brilliant! I keep tellin' Robert he needs to do somethin' creative you nah. He's up the stairs playing Playstation! ROBERT? ROBERT?

ROB.   I'm 'ere dad! Alright mate. Dad y'alright to lend us 20p?

HOWARD.   Wha' you wan' 20p for boy? I gi' yer 20p yesterday.

ROB.   I know but we're going swimmin' again, I just need it for the lockers.

HOWARD.   You tink I'm made o' money Robert? Tom, will you be wantin' 20p for the locker?

TOM.   Yeah please, if that's alright Howard.

HOWARD.   No problem, but I'll be wanting that back when you're rich and famous boy!

—

TOM.   Mate, your dad is a proper laugh!

As we cross the path through Bedford field,
And walk towards Walkden baths.

But as we approach Parrfold Park we stop in our tracks,
Cuz we've seen three lads, all with their hoods up.
Cut the laughs in a flash, cuz that's not a good look,
In the City of Salford. Always on edge.
I bow my head down and mumble to Rob under my breath…

TOM.   Honestly mate I hope these don't start.

He's like,

ROB.   Nah don't worry, you're with me, and I'm hard!

TOM.   Turns out, it was just our mates being silly
Then I hear shouts, a familiar sound

BOYS.   Eyyar Gilly!

Oi Oi. You boys were shitting yourselves.

TOM.   Nah we weren't, shut the fuck up.

As I look up,
At Lee, Nick and Sav
Who's the last to take down his hood.
And as he does,
I notice his had his haircut and it looks
proper good, so I say...

TOM.   Yer hair looks shit mate.

Cuz my role within this group is piss take,
And it's usually Sav who's the one getting
ripped,
For being scrawny, until he started getting
ripped,
Working out everyday and gettin' proper fit,
And now he's managed to get with this bird
Annette who's proper fit!

Then there's Nick.
Mr. Nice, slick.
Won't wear any item of clothing without a
Nike tick.

In year six he was asked to take his pic,
For an advertising campaign, paying him
fifty quid.
I remember at the time him thinking it
wouldn't be too bad,
Until we saw the advert was for gay
adoption,
And he adopted the name 'Two Dads'.

At the time he was buzzing,
Like "yeah yeah you see that mate? You see
that? Easy money"
Which is funny,
Cuz I don't think he realized the hard work
Was actually gonna come much later,
When that advert then got featured every
single week in our local paper,
Hitting the floor, of every door in the entire
estate,
And he'd have walk into assembly the next
day,
To eight hundred giggles & strew laughs,
All chanting

He's got TWO DAD'S.   He's got TWO
DAD'S.

Then there's Lee.

Now before he met me, he was a bit a loner,
Joined our group became a complete stoner.
Keeps himself to himself, quiet most of the
time
But then he'll just come out with these
random lines like...

LEE.   Eyyar Ggyyillleh, you ever faxed a bird??

Lee laughs hysterically to himself in silence.

TOM.   Then laughs like it's the funniest thing he's
ever heard.
But I wouldn't change these boys for the
world,
(I'd change the world for these boys)
With my raps

14

Say anything in class, just to make 'em laugh.

LEE.   Eyar! Gggyilleh, do that one you did the other night when you stayed round ours.

TOM.   Nah but seen as though we're in the park,
I could spit a few *playground* bars!
Cuz I just took Sav's new girl to *see saw*,
It was a *roundabout* nine,
My hands *slide* up her thighs til I was touching her *zip-line*,
Being careful not to *climb in frame* we did rude things,
It's a*maze*ing the way she puts up with my mood, *swings!*

The boys all celebrate.

BOYS.   Ohhhhhhhh!!

TOM.   Two whole hours in the park, spitting bars,
Til suddenly out of nowhere the parks gone dark,
Out the corner of our eyes we spot these guys from afar,
Next minute one of 'em jumps the fence and says...

CHEEKY.   Eyar! You. You got a cig?

TOM.   I look to my left at Lee. Look back at his boggled eyes and say...

Sorry, you talking to him or me?

CHEEKY.	YOU! You best have fucking cig for me there!
TOM.	Nah. I don't smoke mate.
CHEEKY.	Yeah you fucking do. I seen you smoking.
TOM.	Nah honestly mate that weren't me.
CHEEKY.	What you lying for? You scared of me? Look at yer, you're proper fucking scared aren't yer? Do you know who I am?
TOM.	Yeah. You're 'Cheeky'.
CHEEKY.	Yeah I am. And d'yer know why they call me Cheeky?
TOM.	I dunno mate, is it cuz you're-
CHEEKY.	CHEEKY. YEAH! I'M FUCKING DEAD CHEEKY ME MATE! Now you best give me a fucking cig!
TOM.	I can tell from the smell that he's well pissed. Pissed my self. My self- Esteem shattered. Look for my boys on the left, But they've all left, Next Cheeky swings his left And I'm left, Lying bruised and battered. By this boggled-eyed guy Who decided that I'd Looked at him Funny

16

How your mates,
Can run away,
In your times of
Need,
To get back to my phat stash of
Weed
All over my
Self-
Ish
TWATS!

Said you'd be there but when it came to it
lads
Not one of you had my
Backs
Killing from where he stuck his heel in

LEE.   It'll heal in a week mate.

TOM.   Yer weak, mate!

I stood and took a punch, while you all run
off through the trees eh?

Yeah, go on. Fuck off!

Tom paces. Gets out his mobile. Calls home.

TOM.   Alright Mum. What we having for tea?
Argh I fucking hate Turkey Twizzlers!
Sorry.
Oh yeah I did! Right mum you'll never guess
what.
You know that film 'Eden Lake' that I
auditioned for?
The one that's gonna have Michael
Fassbender in it?

17

Michael Fassbender.

Yeah you do, he was in that film '300'.

What pool?

No mum, that's Michael Barrymore!

Well anyway I got a call this morning, and they've offered me a part in it. Yeah I'm dead chuffed.

Yeah, well you never know, it could be my ticket out of here.

No, I know theres nothing wrong with 'ere mum.

Ah thanks.

Nah I don't wanna speak to him.

Alright then put him on.

TOM waits anxiously

Y'alright dad?

Yeah I'm just in the park with the boys.

Well it's nothing really, it's just you know that film that I auditioned for?

Well I got a call this morning... and, they've offered me the part!

I think it's paid yeah.

Yeah I know I do Dad, and I said I'll give it you that back next week-

Yeah I know I do but I still haven't been paid yet so I can't-

Dad, c'mon it's only a fiver.

No I know that's not the point but-

18

I'm not a waste of space Dad, I just haven't...

Dad? Dad?!

TOM paces furiously. HELEN calls. TOM answers.

TOM. Helen, what do you want?
Yeah I know you've been trying to call,
I've just been on the phone to my dad and it keeps going beep beep beep. Well it's pretty fucking annoying to be honest, what do you want?

Oh my god are you still going on about that job interview?
To be honest Helen I don't care. I've got more important things going on in my life at at the minute than you and your stupid fucking...
Helen? Helen?

TOM sits down in a strop. His trainers brush a Capo lying by his feet on the floor. He inquisitively picks it up and fiddles with it. He then spots an acoustic guitar. He picks up the guitar, places the capo on neck of the guitar and strums a chord.

TOM. Sick!

So I've somehow managed to fall out with my family, my girlfriend,
And every single one of my mates, and it's not even three o'clock.

TOM plays a chord progression on the guitar.

I just wanna crawl into bed.

Cuz at least, when I'm asleep
For those few hours I can forget.

But for now...

LONG WALK HOME

I'll take the long walk home
Down Newearth Road
I'm only in a t-shirt
And it's freezing cold
But this road with a smoke is better than home
This road with a smoke is better than home.

Home.
Just one big fight.
Sitting in my room a mess, and it's messing with my
mind.
I walk around the house with my head down, and my
chin it wont lift,
And this feeling in the pit of my stomach it won't shift.
I'd take one of dad's fists over this any day.
Last night I overheard my mum saying to him,
"Well, you never wanted him anyway"
He never wanted me anyway.

And so I'll take the long walk home
Down Newearth Road
I'm only in a t-shirt
And it's freezing cold
But this road, with a smoke, is better than home
But this road, with a smoke, is better than home

I'm nearly back already, think I'll give it another ten,
Go down this ginnel and sit on this bench,
This bench where me and Helen had our first kiss,
It was bliss, a feeling that we've started to miss.

I really do need to start treating her better.
I'm gonna buy her some flowers, and write her a letter,
Telling her why I love her, and I love us being together,
And how I have these mad visions of being with her
forever.

My mates all keep on telling me she's bad news
But I reckon they're just jealous or something,
She cures my blues, she cures my blues,
But whenever I'm out with her lately i'm always in a
mood.
I just need to get out of this place
Out of his space
Before I straight out starting pounding his face
Need to stop pacing around the estate
And work out where all this anger is based
Cuz right now I just feel so out of place
Just keep going out, and getting out of my face,
How come whenever I go out I'm in a rage?
Like last week when I took Helen out on a date.

She's made an effort to look nice in her dress an,
Proper gone all out to make a good impression
The waiters looking at me, and I'm sitting there
stressin',
I'VE GOT AN ISSUE WITH MY SALAD, AND IT
NEEDS a-DRESSING!
I'm obsessing over the small shit,
Like brown skid marks left on the side of a bog,
Everyone is just pissing me off. Everyone is just pissing
me off!

And as I walk in school they're all being rude to me,
Outside the canteen throwing their food at me,
I guess that's why as I'm getting older
I feel like I constantly walk around with a fucking chip
on my shoulder!

And I told her, I wouldn't let all of this get in the way,
I'm in pain, but I know that she's not the one to blame,
My hands have gone numb, looks like its gonna rain,
But I can't face, his face
And so I take

The long walk home
Down Newearth Road
I'm only in a t-shirt and it's freezing cold

But this road, with a smoke, is better than home
This road, with a smoke, is better than home
Said this road, with a smoke, is better than home
One last toke, of my roach, and now i'm...

Home.

Tom puts the guitar down.

TOM.   And I pass my dad on the stairs,
                 There's no words said between us, just
                 stares.

                 And I have this little box room
                 So I go and hide in it.
                 And even though I feel like I'm trapped in a
                 box,
                 I'm always thinking outside of it.

                 Then later that night my mum comes in,
                 I hear him saying he's *washed his hands* of me
                 to her in the *kitchen*
                 And that *sinks* in.
                 Why's he acting so *cold tap*ped in the head,
                 plates smash in the kitchen,
                 I can hear 'em, from my bedroom.

While my mum *soaks* it all up like a *sponge*, screams…

MUM. IT'S SO DRAINING ALWAYS COMPLAINING, ENOUGH ON MY PLATE, JUST WIPE THE SLATE CLEAN!

TOM. And…

MUM. YOU DON'T LOVE ME RIGHT, YOU DON'T EVEN HUG YOUR WIFE

TOM. And you could cut the atmosphere in here, with a *fork and knife*.

So that night… I decide it has to stop.

I go down to the kitchen to get some bottled water,
Open the fridge and see that he's bought a crate.
Then I open the living room door, which feels more like a gate.
He's sat watching Bolton on Match Of The Day.
(Yeah, when we used to be in the fucking premiership)

And I say…

TOM. Dad am I alright to grab a beer and join yer?

Now the wait is excruciating,
I've just been up the stairs pacing,
Debating what I'm gonna say
And the way I'm gonna say it.

23

He doesn't even look at me just stares at the station and says...

DAD.   Yeah, if you give me 50p.

TOM.   Now I'm young,
And I'm stung,
By this miserable cunt
Who blames mum,
For giving me funds
To take up guitar lessons
And after school clubs
Which is the only time I ever feel any good
But he says "tough!"
Cuz money's tight,
And his thinking is black and white.
Has a million reasons for not doing
something before even giving it a try,
And says that I'm just a bum

DAD.   Don't listen to your Mum!
Life's not all about having fun.

TOM.   No it's not
It's just about get cross at how much things cost,
And talking to everyone like you're the boss and saying...

DAD.   You're thick lad!

TOM.   No I'm not dad!

I take a crack to the back of my head

DAD.   I SAID, you're thick lad!

TOM.   No I'm not dad!

Another crack to the back of my head

TOM.   I said, stop!

DAD.   Maths! That's what you wanna do.
Maths is easy, cuz one and one is always two.

TOM.   Yeah but I'm an artist dad.
I play guitar and that.
Maths is not for me,
I'm more like, what about if one and one...
could make three?

DAD.   But one and one doesn't make bloody three!

TOM.   Alright I know, there's no need to go
ballistic.

DAD.   Tom you've only got to look at the statistics.
What you wanna do is not a feasible career,
You need to stop living up there lad, and
start living down here!

TOM.   You're just full of fear,
Scared to take risks,
Don't take it out on me just cuz your jobs
shit,
And you sit at a desk, everyday stressed,
Come home and moan, all depressed,
Then try and tell me that you know best?

DAD.   Alright Tom, you fuck off and do your
stupid little film
And write your stupid little songs,

But don't be coming back to me when it all goes wrong.

TOM.   Please dad.
I know you don't agree with my path.
But this isn't just something I'm doing for a laugh
I'm willing to graft.
And I know it won't be easy but I'll work hard for it.
Now I didn't even want a beer,
I was just offering you an olive branch,
And all you can think about is how much to charge me for it?
You actually wanna charge me for it?

DAD.   Hang on, Tom, let me get my receipt,
Right, so these beers cost me 12.23p
You divide that by the 15, that's around 82p each
So what I'm offering you for, at 50p a can, is pretty fucking cheap!

Not to mention the petrol I had to put in my car.
And unless you're bloody disabled now you've gotta pay to park!
You've gotta pay your way if you're living at home still!
And I take it you haven seen the state of our phone bill?
You expecting me to pay for that as well?
Here's a spreadsheet I've devised on Excel.
It outlines all the costs covered in our tariff,
And the calls you've been making that have taken it over that balance.

So on the twentieth of February at four
thirty eight,
You called the doctors-

TOM. I was ill.

DAD. It's a premium rate!

Then again here on the twenty second,
You made a call to a mobile number, for two
seconds!

Tom takes the phone bill off his DAD.

TOM. What? Oh right, I think that's Helen's
number, I was probably just prank calling
her so she could call me back.

DAD. Prank call? What do you think this is...
bloody trigger happy TV?

TOM. All right! You don't have to make
everything so tense. So how much do I owe
you?

DAD. Eighty four pence.

TOM laughs

TOM. Is that it?

DAD. Is that it?

*TOM'S DAD violently grabs TOM by the throat and strangles
him.*

DAD.   Is that it? Is that it? Yes that is fucking it lad!

TOM escapes.

TOM.   And I run, and slam the door shut at the front
And I run from that cunt
Face
And I race
Out of my estate
At a pace
As tears stream down my face,
I'm weak,
Stamping each one of my feet
So that my knees can feel a sharp pain,
I'm a wreck, and my neck,
I can still feel it,
As I run through the night across Bedford Field
And Parrfold Park
In the pitch dark,
And the cold,
And at the end of this guinell is the East Lancs Road.
The A580,
Which is known to be one of the most dangerous roads in the whole of Walkden
I should probably walk then,
But I don't,
I race
At a pace
Towards this fuck off motorway,
Where only the other day,
Lauren Tennant a girl who lived on my street
And went to my school the year below me,

Stepped out too soon, after consuming a few too many Reefs,
I'm not lying,
Look it up on Google,
She was 14,
She was hit full force by a Ford,
Flipped over the back of that, into the path of more,
Oncoming traffic,
Then got clipped by another car as that tried to swerve past her,
Before her entire body, became entangled underneath a HGV lorry,
And she was pronounced dead at the scene,
And from what I heard from the people what seen,
There was nothing left of her, she was split into bits
And to be honest right now I envy that bitch.
Cuz I would love to never have to go back to that shit,
And get rid of this pain,
So I'll run and I'll run,
Until someone screams my fucking name.

TOM!!

TOM halts. HOWARD appears.

HOWARD.   TOM? Where you running to at this time boy?

TOM.   Oh, erm, nowhere, just getting a bit of exercise Howard.

HOWARD.   Hmm. Exercise? I've just been getting my exercise with Mrs Howard. You know what I'm saying boy? She be walking like John Wayne!

TOM.   Wow.
Well, I'll have to let Rob know. What you doing out here?

HOWARD.   I'm just watering me trees y'nah.

TOM.   You've been watering those trees for a while now haven't you Howard. Where are they?

HOWARD.   Well they're just seeds at the moment. But this time next year you'll be lookin' at a rainforest. You just got to have a bit of patience!
Here, you wanna help me give them a liccle sprinkle?

TOM.   Yeah ok.

TOM takes hold of the hosepipe. HOWARD places a hand on TOM's shoulder. TOM holds back tears.

HOWARD.   Is evertin' ok?

TOM nods.

HOWARD.   You know the one thing about trees. Nomatter how old they get, they never stop growing!

TOM.   Cool.

HOWARD. Don't worry, everytin' gonna be alright. You just got to have a bit of patience.

(And you got to work on that Jamaican accent; it's all over the fucking place!)

-

Music starts.

Boundary Stone Pub

TOM.

In the Boundary Stone Pub
It's so good!
In the Boundary Stone Pub,
It's all love,
In the Boundary Stone Pub
We'll get fucked
In the Boundary Stone, in the Boundary Stone!

TOM heads over to the micprohone and amp and uses it as a Karaoke Machine. He impersonates Jamie T.

Yeah, the Boundary Stone Pub
Is so good.
In the Boundary Stone Pub
It's all love,
In the Boundary Stone Pub
We'll get fucked
In the Boundary Stone, in the Boundary Stone!

TOM snaps out of it.

Since the age of fourteen
This place has been the place of our dreams
And now we're all in our late teens

But still haven't quite turned eighteen
And my short legs and baby face means
I don't stand a chance
But Two-Dads has devised a plan
To raid both his dads wardrobes for a suit and tie

So I head back to mine, and put on my Dads shirt
And we all act like 'yeah mate, we've just come from
work'
But I'm in trouble
Cuz I'm the only one of us without any stubble

NICK.   Aww, imagine we get in there mate!

LEE.   Yeah, there's gonna be bare fanny in there mate!

SAV.   Yeah, we'll easily pull in there mate!

TOM.   Yeah mate. I can't wait!

I've heard every single girl in there's fit
And the girl to guy ratio, is always an even split
So we're guaranteed to pull for sure
And as we all rock up at the front door

Lee says...

LEE.   Eyyar! Gggyilleh, you go in first!

TOM.   No! Why?

LEE.   Cuz you look the worst. If you can get served, then we'll definitely get served.

TOM.   Thanks mate.

And as we pass the fruit machines, and the 20 inch TV
screens
And I think that might just be the girl of my dreams,
I say...

Music stops.

TOM.   Can I have four pints of Fosters please?

KAREN.   Have you got yer ID's?

TOM.   Err, no but we've just come from work,
                    that's why we're all wearing suits.

KAREN.   Well you can be wearing what you want
                    love, but if you 'ant got yer ID's I can't serve
                    yer.

SAV.   Fuck sake Gilleh!

Music starts.

TOM.
Excuse me, if I could just have a minute, Karen,
That's a very lovely name
If I could just explain, basically, we are all underage

TOM adopts a musical theatre approach.

But we've been dreaming of this for a very long time,
And it really would be such a shame
To be turned away at this very late stage in the game.

KAREN.   You've got no chance love.

TOM.

Alright, look, I know the guys behind all look about five
And it might seem like they're all really nice,
But they're actually all really dark characters Karen
And if you don't pour me a pint
Well they've all got knives
And when we get outside,
They've threatened to end my life!

And I don't think you want that resting on your
conscience, do you Karen?

And I'm already having a lot of trouble at home,
And I'm feeling really lost and lonely
And... oh my god, is that, Tony? Tony!
You're the manager right?
Ah it's so great to finally put a name to a face
Just me and my mates, were wondering if you could be
our saviour?
I promise we'll be on our best behavior
We'll even pay yer, double the price of every pint

SAV.   Nah we fucking wont!

TOM.

Yes we fucking will Tony.
So nice to meet you, I'm Tom Gill, Tony.

You know, its funny
We've only just met,
And yet,
I feel like I've known you all of my life!

You're not just some misogynistic guy that works behind
the bar
I bet you're really into the arts aren't you Tony?
And you're just running this pub

So you can save up to put on that new spoken word
musical you've been devising
Exploring themes of working class masculinity- aren't
you?

TOM acquires an American accent

Hey Tony! "When you meet a guy reach for starts in the
sky, you can bet that he's doing it for some..."

What's that from? Its Guys and Dolls Tony!

OK OK! Calm down Tony, there's no need to get mad at
me,
Hey, isn't it funny how your name contains two parts of
the human anatomy... 'Toe' 'knee'?

Ok I'm sorry Tony. I'm sorry.
I've just loved musicals ever since I played Oliver in
High School
And so sometimes I just feel the need to break into a
song for absolutely no fucking reason.

Now please.
Can I have four pints?
My mouth is so dry
You're such a nice guy.
Tony!

-

The boys stand outside the Boundary Stone pub.

SAV.   Fuck sake Gilly.

TOM.   What? What've I done?

SAV.   Well we'd of all got served if it wasn't for you, why d'you have to be so small?

TOM.   Oh well I'm sorry I didn't inherit the right jeans!

LEE.   You're not even wearing jeans Gilly.

NICK.   This is proper shit this. I'm going home me.

LEE.   Yeah me too.

TOM.   What, is everyone just going home now then yeah?

SAV.   Yeah, no point staying out here is there? The night's ruined.

TOM.   Fuckin' hell boys, the night's not ruined.
It weren't even that good in there anyway, there was hardly anyone in it.
The nights ruined, have you heard yerself?
The night's not ruined, the night's what you make it.
It's not about where you are is it? It's about who you're with.

SAV.   Yeah exactly, and we're with you.

TOM.   Right someone give us a beat... Lee, give me a beat.

LEE throws down his cigarette and beatboxes.

TOM.   ONE, I'll tell yer bout my girl I broke her heart into TWO

36

Got really angry now I'm tryin' to talk it through,
I'm banging on her house but she wont answer the door
I knocked at number THREE, I think she lives at number FOUR

Pickup the FIVE, to the SIX, to the EIGHT
I'm no good at maths dad so just give me a break
I spend most of my time just learning how to rhyme
And being too mouthy- like in a sixty-NINE

Pickup up the TEN, to the ELEVEN, to the TWELVE
I'm working at Tesco stacking up shelves,
But I wanna be an actor that'd be the dream
"Where d'yer keep the bread mate?"
"Isle THIRTEEN"

Pickup the FOURTEEN, to the FIFTEEN, to the SIXTEEN
Get a call through from my agent Christine
Got a part in a film, need to learn seven scenes
This thing called 'Eden Lake' about a gang of SEVEN-TEEN'S

Pick-up the EIGHTEEN, to the NINETEEN...

Now we're TWENTY!

-

And instead standing outside the Boundary
Stone Pub, rapping shit
We're finally old enough to sit inside the
pub...

Chatting shit.

Inside the Boundary Stone Pub.

LEE.   Ggggyillehhh... you ever been in a film
called 'Evil Snakes'?

TOM.   It was 'Eden Lake'.

LEE.   Eyyar, Ggggillehhh... you ever been in a
film called *(mimicking TOM)* 'Eden Lake',
and then never been in any other films, ever
again?

TOM.   Thanks for reminding me mate.

LEE.   That's ok. Gggyilleh, you ever been in a film
called Evil Snakes, where the rest of the cast
go on to have really successful acting careers,
while you just stack shelves in Tesco and
write poetry to your fat ex- girlfriend?

TOM.   Sorry mate, what was the last film that you
were in?

LEE.   Just that one I did with ye mam!

LEE laughs hysterically in silence.

LEE.   *(Whispering)* Gilly? Gilly? Gilly? Gilly?
(Shouting) Gyyyileeeehh!

TOM.   Fuck off!

LEE.   Alright Gilly! Is it cuz your Dad doesn't love
                   yer?

TOM.   Seriously Lee I'm warning you now, fuck off!

TOM sits back in his chair.

> -
> I'm sitting here thinking, it's mad with age
> it's
> Like so much changes, yet nothing changes.
>
> I mean, Lee's still just a complete fucking
> tool.
> Nick still gets called 'Two Dad's' like he was
> back in school
> But then... well then there's Sav!

These Days

Sav was never a bad lad just a bit of a dick,
Now he's addicted to
Smacks his kids,
Kids with us lads and the other Dads that he
Spots,
All over his face
As he sits in the same
Places all his hopes and dreams on the league
Stares up at the screen and flares up at his team and
screams
"What the fuck was that?? That should have been me
Me gran's ninety-three and even she'd of put it in the
back of the net"
Annette,
Sits next to him,

She's his next of kin
She dunt really talk at all,
Just sits and necks her gin
Every now he'll turn around and ask her who she's
messaging
But the beds the only time I expect she ever lets him
IN-
habited this pub like it's their own home
It's the only place we've ever known
Run by 'Big-Tone'
Funny how he called the pub the Boundary Stone
And now everyone just stays within its 'boundaries'
'stoned'

And these days
There's nothing left here for me, mate
And money dunt grow on trees, mate
And somehow I'm gonna make mine

But I'm hurt, loads
Walking down past Birch, Road
My friends are stuck in that work, mode
It's their lives I've gotta live mine

Now Sav's an addict with a habit, and we know he's been
at it
Vicious with his addiction that's why our mate 'Nick
named' him Savage
Knows he shouldn't do this line but this time
'Saville/Sav'll' risk it
Got all these under lying issues and still thinks the
'Jim'll/Gym'll fix it'
But no matter how much he's been working out
His relationship with Annette still isn't working out
He feels like every days just the same at work. In. Out.
But says he's looking for a new job, working out of town.

And when he gets it, his life turns around,
He comes down the pub now, looking proper sound,
Got a little spring in his step like nothing could bring
him down,
Except for what Annette's been up to when he's not been
around.

But I've never seen Sav this happy, so I'm not gonna
spoil it
But we all know she's been knobbing some other bloke in
the toilet
And that's not some fabricated rumor designed to amuse
us all
Cuz while it was happening I was sat crapping in the
next cubical.

Step on the toilet seat, look over and see
Can't believe it, it's only fucking LEE

LEE.   Alright Gyyggilleh! You ever fingered a wasp??

TOM goes over to the mic and amp and uses it as a Karaoke Machine. Impersonating Oasis.

TOM.

And these days
There's nothing left here for me, mate
And money dunt grow on trees, mate
And somehow I'm gonna make mine

But I'm hurt, loads
Walking down past Birch, Road
My friends are stuck in that work, mode
It's their lives I've gotta live mine

Tom drops the mic.

Then comes the day of the big game
Derby day, pub crawl
Sav's in the pub
But he hasn't said fuck all,
Then he picks up a chair,
Comes and sits with us all
Says he knows about his missus cheating with Lee
While we watch the football

Then bang on cue Lee walks in
And we all know what happens next
Sav vexed turns back and picks up his pint of Becks
Walks straight over to Lee and cracks him over the back
of his head
So his neck, like the rest of Manchester's now covered in
red

As the fight breaks out through the doors, and onto the
street
Everyone's rushing and pushing as Lee stumbles over his
own feet
And he falls, head first
Onto the curb of the pavement
And I'm looking at everyone's faces
And they're all laughing,
Lapping this up like its entertainment!

I run over to Lee and drag him up onto his knees,
Shout over to two-dads,

TOM.   Eyar lad, go get your keys!
                      We need to get him to a hospital mate,
                      It's not far

                      And he's like

NICK.   Nah, I'm not getting fucking blood in me car!

And I'm thinking

These days
There's nothing left here for me, mate
And money dunt grow on trees, mate
And somehow im gonna make mine

As Lee screams "it hurts loads"
I'm looking down at his burst, nose
I'm thinking could this be worse? No
It's their lives I've gotta live mine,

And I think now's the time
To leave this city
I'm gonna leave this city
I'm gonna leave this city

This city of mine.

-

Part 2. London

Phone rings.

CHARLIE. *(On the phone)* Three hundred quid?
Nah nah nah you're gonna need a lot more
than three hundred quid mate. Yeah, you
can't even buy a fucking beer for that down
here.
Nah I can't get you a job at mine mate I've
just been fired int' I?
Yeah, you know that manager I was
shagging? Oi Tom this is well funny right. I
dunno if you've ever had it with a bird but
where they squirt right, yeah course you
have, well she was a proper squirter geez!
Yeah and last week, my Danny come in the
pub and she was in the back on lunch, and
he was like, 'Oi Chaz, how's it been going
with that manager bird?' I was like 'yeah
yeah, I made her piss the bed last night dint
I?' turn around and she's only fucking stood
behind me geez. Yeaaaaah. Yeah but she's
like a proper woman man. Yeah she dont
find shit like that funny. Yeah it's well funny
aint it! Oi, Tom my Danny runs a call centre.
Yeah they're always looking for people man.
I done it for a while, it's well shit, it's a job
though ain't it. Yeah that's alright you can
just come and stay at mine for a bit. Yes
mate, this is gonna be quality!

TOM. So just like that, I'm living in Charlie's flat,
Thinking this is mental this.
I've only been in London a week
And I've already started going *up*, at the end
of my senten*ces*.

44

Now Charlie's heavy on the drugs
But he's light on life, and that's exactly
what I need right about now.
We had a sick time on working on that film
Eden Lake together,
And now look at us. Fucking flatmates!

To be fair the call centre is proper shit.
And I could easily find another job.
I should quit.
But I don't and the reason is this.

-

On the first day, she came up and said,

BETH.   Hey, who are you?

I'm like

TOM.   I'm Tom. I'm new.

BETH.   First day and your late?

TOM.   Yeah, well I've just moved here haven't I?
Still trying to get my head round the tubes.

BETH.   Oh it's well easy. I could always show you
around if you like?

TOM.   Yeah all right... what you doing tonight?

Her name was Beth.
Beth Green.
Asked me if I fancied a drink with her in
east.
I said *Shore-ditch* your stuff and we'll leave.

We got on the overground at *Hackney Wick*
Shadwell nice eyes, and *Wapping* big tits.

Said there was a pub she knew she loved but
didn't know which way to go,
I said I'm new to London but maybe this
White-chap-el know?

We asked this guy for directions
But he sent us walking in the wrong
direction
For about a *Mile End* ing back in
*Hackne*eded to stop off for some cash at a
Bank.
She said she only lived *Em-bank-ment*
We could just have cheap laugh back at her
flat.
So with that, we went to an off license
To buy some Corona's with *Lime-*
House was empty when we got back so I felt
relaxed enough to chat.

She asked me what it was I did, I said I act,
infact,
Way back I did a film with Michael
Fassbender earning a wack.
Everywhere we went we got escorted and
Now instead of learning lines, I seem to
spend more time snorting them.

She said, "What, are you well into your
drugs?"
I said, "When I'm not a busy bee I do love a
buzz"
She turns her back and pulls out a big bag of
magic mush
Tells me to trust says they're good

Her mate Mark got it.
Said I'd never really been in to the hallucinogenics just narcotics
But FUCK IT
Sometimes it's just nice to get away from life's hassles,
Next minute I'm seeing mad shit like *Elephants and Castles*.

The flat becomes this *Manor House* with barbed wires.
Then a religious *Temple* full of these *Black friars* with *Oval* heads.
She said "you alright Tom? You're not looking your best?"
I said, "I think this stuff's sending me west"

Started turning *White, City* spinning
I could barley talk
She said, "You sound funny",
I said "It's just cuz I'm from the North."
She said, "of course *Wood Green* sort you out?"
I said, "I reckon that's a good shout"

And we sat and smoked for about two hours til we were both
High-Buried the sick feeling in my stomach inside.

Then later that night conversation turns deep.
Started talking about our families
Seven Sisters she never sees.
It all started with her Dad, who would cheat,
On her Mum, and beat her up,

And speak to her like she
Was a piece, of dirt on his feet.

So to help her deal with it, she started
smoking weed,
But her sisters are all religious or summit
and disagree,
And even though she was the one who chose
to leave
Now she feels disowned.
And whenever they agree to meet she turns
up *Leyton-stoned*.
So they've all written her off.
She says she trying, but she's lost.
Her mum made her hate the thought of love-
ma*King-Cross*
Because when it comes to sex she always
feels *Euston*
Has to force herself to do it.

I said I can relate to a lot of those feeling of
family isolation
And all the hate too,
Cuz I've been through it.

It's like listening to myself,
It's kind of painful to see
But if it's any consolation
You're an *Angel* to me!

-

Counselling room.

TOM.   And every time she touches me, It makes my
                 skin crawl.

48

I hate the sense of her breath on my neck, as
she tries to comfort me.
Her kisses smother me.

It's coming up to six months now.
It was great at the start.
Really great.
She's different to the girls back home.
She gentle, and warm, and kind,
And she dunt mind if I have no money, or a
fancy car, and things like that.

Like, it was her birthday a couple of months
back,
And I was so skint, so I could only really
afford to get her one present.
So I bought her these goalie gloves.
You shoulda seen her face.
"What are these?"
I said they're goalie gloves.
Cuz you're a 'keeper'

She is.
She's funny, she's smart... she's a really a
good listener.
Which is just as well really, because I just
talk at her.

Scream at her.

Which is why I've come here.

But she just makes me so fucking angry.
Why's she so happy all the time?
She's so light about everything. And
everyone.
Everyone's her friend.

Everyone's not her fucking friend.
She's naïve.
She says "Don't worry, it'll all come out in
the wash"
But it won't, will it?

I can't stand her smile,
She has the most beautiful smile.
Like if you were design a smile,
But I want to wipe it off her face.
Is that bad?
I want to punch the fucking teeth from her
mouth.
What's she got to smile about?

Her sisters don't speak to her.
Her Dad's a fucking cheat.
All her friends are doing really well in their
careers, she's not.
Oh and her fucking friends!
Why does she hang round with posh spoilt
twats?
She's not even like that!
They're all just like
"Hey guys, oh my gawd, I am literally so
poor today.
I'm like so homeless. I literally can't even
afford to buy quinoa. Bluerugh!
Yah but I'm so looking forward to my
holiday with Mum and Dad next week... "

Yeah, fuck off!

Sorry.

Anyway, the thing that I wanted to talk to
you about.

Last week, me and Beth had quite a big row.
And we were supposed to be going to her
mate's house party together the next day.
And I really just did not feel like going.
Like, I couldn't think of anywhere I would
want to be less than surrounded by people
But I knew how much is meant to her.
So I went.
And I get chatting to this lad!

-

House Party.

BART.   Hey! You're Beth's boyfriend right? You're
the "actor"?

TOM.   Yeah, that's me.

BART.   Cool sweet man, sweet... so what've you
been in?

TOM.   Not a lot recently. Well, nothing that you'd
know anyway.

BART.   Cool cool, I bet you've been in the job centre
though haven't you? Only messing, only
messing. So where is it your from orginally?

TOM.   I'm from Manchester. Well, Salford.

BART.   Ah Manchester! I fucking love Manchester.
Yeah no, I used to work up in Manchester
actually, yeah, fucking great music scene
isn't it? I'm a big Ian Curtis fan myself.

TOM.   Ah right cool. Who's that?

51

BART.   Ian Curtis? Like, the lead singer of Joy Division?

Oh c'mon, are you thick or something you must you must have heard of Joy Division? They're like one of the greatest bands of the 80's.

TOM.   What did you just say?

BART.   Joy division? One of the greatest bands of the 80's

TOM.   Nah before that... before that, what did you say?

BART.   I, erm, I can't remember

TOM.   Nah nah nah, don't you fucking play games with me lad.
Before that. Before the 'Joy Dvision', go on, what did you say?

BART.   Ah dude. You mean about you being thick or something, was that it?

TOM.   Was that it?

Mirroring his DAD in the earlier scene, TOM grabs BART by his neck

TOM.   Was that it?! Yes that was fucking it lad!

Tom in a fit of rage beats up BART and strangles him almost to death.

-

Counselling Room.

TOM. And all I can see is his eyes. But it's not his eyes I'm seeing.
I'm not seeing his eyes; I'm seeing *his* eyes.
And I want to stick a knife in them.
I want to steal the life from them.
I want those eyes red
I want those eyes bled
I want those eyes dead.
I can hear Beth scream. I can hear her stream of tears
But this is years...
There's spilt beer
But it's not here.
None of it's here
It's just me and him.
It's just me.
And *him*.

Look, is there any chance I can get some sleeping pills or something I just need...

I just really need...

TOM can't find the words. He picks up his guitar.

<u>*My mind*</u>

I just need to get my head down
I need to get my head round
All of these things, haven't been to sleep, for weeks

And when I sleep I can't wake up
I wake up I can't face up
To anybody else
I'm talking to myself

Cuz it's only me and my mind
And my mind, can't decide
Whether it wants to let me live
It's stripped me of wings

It's telling me that I can't get up early,
It's telling me that I'm not worthy
It's telling me I'm dirty
It's telling me i'm better off just staying off and being on
my own, ill
It's catastrophising and making mountains out of
molehills

It's standing right beside me, wherever I run it'll find me
It's telling me I might be
Able to escape with the aid of those pills
But it'll come back and hit me harder than my father did
and he'll
Be there to trip me up wherever I go
He'll tell everyone to stay away from me that I know
Whatever I do it'll turn out bad
This constant voice in my head, sounds just like the voice
of my dad

And it's telling me that I'm too old to be hugged,
Telling me that I'll never amount to much
Telling me that it's all my fault
And it never lets me enjoy anything
Without finding and reminding me
Of all of my faults

It's spitting in my face, I'm begging it to leave
But it's got its legs around my neck, sat on my chest
So I can't breath
It's looming over me at work, trying to inhibit me
Telling me I'm dirt, that's why it's having a dig at me

I run away and escape through the drugs
But when I come down, from all those hugs in the clubs
And I'm fucked
There'll always be that grudge
Cuz where do you run, when you're unloved?
And I'm spitting right back in its face, as it tells me I'm a
slob
"Look at the state of you mate, can't even hold down a
proper job
You're late for work again, one more strike and you're
finished
You look like shit, why don't you take five minute and…"

Get your head down
I need to get my head round
All of these things, haven't been to sleep, for weeks

And when I sleep I can't wake up
I wake up I can't face up
To anybody else
I'm talking to myself

Cuz it's only me and my mind
And my mind, can't decide
Whether it wants to let me live
It's stripped me of my wings.

-

TOM.   So I agree to meet Beth in the cafe on the corner of Forest Hill station
I order us some cheesy chips, but she looks weak and tells me she can't eat

BETH.   I don't want you're fucking chips Tom. What was all that about at the party? You do realise you could've killed him!

TOM.   Yeah well, he was being a dick

BETH.   Tom they're my mates.

TOM.   Nah they ain't. What about Grace? She your
             mate?

BETH.   Yeah, she's one of my best

TOM.   Was she one of your best mates when I
             fucked her?

             I'm looking in her eyes
             Trying to get a rise
             She cries
             But she doesn't get angry
             This was the thing about Beth
             She just didn't have it in her
             She handled everything with poise, and
             dignity, and

BETH.   Grace?
             Is that true about her? And why would you
             do that Tom?

TOM.   Because everyone in this life is a cunt, that's
             why
             You can't trust no one
             Everyone's just out for themselves.

             To my surprise to my surprise
             She dries her eyes
             To my surprise, to my surprise,
             She puts her hands on mine,
             And says,

BETH.   Relationships are like plants Tom.

You've got to look after them babe.
You've gotta nurture them, in order for them to grow.
Just know, that if you stop looking after a plant eventually over time,
It's gonna die,
And I'm really sorry but I think this relationship has died.

No no no, I don't want you to contact me again, not for a long while.
I hope one day our paths will cross and I can look at you and smile,
But for me, this just isn't right,
I loved you
Smash out life.

To my surprise, to my surprise
She takes her hands off of mine
To my surprise, to my surprise
She picks her bag up off the side
And to my surprise, to my surprise,
She walks out of my life
To my surprise to my surprise,
She walks out of my life

Tom watches her go. Sadly. He snaps out of it.

TOM.   Yeah well I want my fucking top back!

                  -

Train sounds.

TOM.   *(On the phone)* Alright mum.
                  Yeah I'm alright, listen, I'm just on a train if it cuts out.

I'm gonna be home in ten minutes.
Well I can ring you back then yeah. But like
I said I'm gonna be home in ten minutes.
Sorry, what don't you understand?
Yeah I am on a train home.
Home. Home
Yeah! What? Your sons coming home. You
not excited? You should be.
Nah nah nah, you don't need to check with
him.
It's him that I'm coming to see.

-

Doorbell rings.

Home.

DAD.   Right Tom.
Me and your mum have agreed.
You can get your stuff.
Then you leave.

TOM.   I don't need any stuff. I've got everything I
need.

DAD.   Well then you can leave.

TOM.   No.

DAD.   I said leave.

TOM.   And I said no

DAD.   This is my house lad, I SAID go

TOM explodes, beating his chest.

58

TOM.   I SAID.I SAID. I SAID.

TOM regains composure.

(And I said)

TOM pulls some seeds from his pocket. Sprinkles them onto the floor. Holds one up to the light.

> If you plant a seed Dad,
> In a positive *light*,
> *Nurture* it in a steady environment
> And give it *time*.
>
> Let it find its *roots* in a *warm space* that it needs,
> Set it apart from all the other seeds,
> It can *blossom* into a *full-grown tree*.
>
> But if you put it not in a *greenhouse*
> In a dark house,
> Treat it like the *dirt* that it's surrounded by
> And *suck it dry*.
> *Soil* it and *dampen* it, too many times,
> It'll grow... ugly, like me.
>
> And I've been *wilting* away amongst the *weeds* and *dog shit*.
> Weed heads and dog shit friends
> Who don't have the *minerals* for you
> Unless there snorting f*ertilizer*
> Met a beautiful *flower*
> But I just flirt and lie to her.
>
> "You'll never *bare fruit*"
> Firmly *planted* in my soul.
> Maybe I'll hang on that *oak* across the road.

It's cold
Sitting in this *rubble* in the dark,
Wishing I could be swept away like the other
leaves in the park
But nah, I'm just that lone *nettle*
The one that gets *stick*.
Stay away from that one it's a trick,
A little *prick*,
But where does that *stem* from?

Cuz I've been growing pains, ever since those
school days
Outside the school gates and it's getting
harder
"I'll pick you up a 3 o' clock Tom
Don't ever be like your father"

But it's like I can't escape your voice,
dragging me down
All I wanted, just for once was for you to say
you were proud
And now,
While your *son* should be out there *shining*,
He doesn't *reign*, he *pours*
And I've been carrying all of this on my
back Dad,
Like you used to carry me on yours.

But fuck that chapter of the book
I'm finally opening up,
To that hole in my soul where I soldered it
shut and
Now I'm showing change!

Y'know the other day, I was in Morrisons
And I went to grab the last sandwich that
was in the reduced section.

It's a great way of saving money that by the way Dad.
And I seen this man eyeing it up, and I think to myself "Nah that's mine",
And as we both go to grab it at the same time,
I get there just before him. Almost snatching it from his hand.

"You little fucker" he growls.
Red in the face.
He's red of face, and he tells me to move out of his way,
And I tell him to move out of mine,
"I can stand where I want mate it's not a crime",
Which provokes a rise and he get right up in my face
And launches a tirade of abuse my way.

Purple now.
He's screaming at me in purple,
But I'm not there anymore.
I could be anyone.
See he's not mad with me.
He's not even mad about the sandwich.
I know that because, it's like looking at my own reflection,
It's like looking at you Dad,
And instead of telling him to go fuck himself,
Do you know what I do?
I put that sandwich back.
And I apologize for being a twat.

"I'm sorry mate", I say
"You have it, it's yours. But this isn't about a sandwich is it?"

And I just ask him straight,

Mate

Mirroring HOWARD in part one.

"Is everything ok?"

Suddenly the colour seeps out of his face.
His whole posture changes, he deflates.

"I'm so sorry mate", he says
"I've just been waiting on some news and
I've been anxious all week"

I say that's ok. I understand. I get that too.
I think we all do. It's normal.

He throws me a smile and tells me to take
care.
And I leave that situation feeling warm. And
fuzzy.
And I think to myself.
Everyone's the same aren't they? Everyone
has they're own story.

Maybe that lad at that party wasn't being a
dick?
I mean, no, he was a bit.
But maybe I already assumed he was gonna
be a dick.
So I didn't even try!
Maybe I was giving off a cold, disinterested
vibe.
Actually, maybe I caused that fight.

And even if he was being a dick,

Maybe all he needed was to be thrown a
smile.
Or to feel wanted.
And valued.
And respected.
Maybe that's all anyone really wants Dad.
Maybe that's all Mum wants Dad.

Y'know when I first left here,
I thought London was going to solve
everything.
I thought it was the answer.
But it's not about where you are is it?
It's about who you're with.

And I'm with this guy.

And I spend a lot of time with him.
Maybe I should learn to be with him.
Maybe I should learn how to treat him,
And then he can treat others the same way.
Maybe I just need to love him first.

TOM clocks a tree outside the window.

You know the one thing I learnt about trees
when I was younger Dad?
"No matter how old they get, they never
stop growing"

Well I'm a fucking tree then.
And you might have chipped away at the
bark,
You might have snapped off the branches,
And torn off the leaves.

But you will never cut me down.

63

TOM's DAD desperately fights back tears.

DAD.   Have you finished?

TOM nods.

DAD.   Right.
              Well get your stuff, and fuck off!

              -

TOM.   And so that's it. Now life goes on.

              Things start to look up again. I'm a little less
              jaded.
              The colours start to come back. Where once
              they had faded.
              I mean some days are a struggle still, but
              some days are good.
              I get offered the chance to travel the world
              doing a job that I love.
              I stand much taller these days. If only Beth,
              could see how much I've grown.
              I'm in a new relationship now, with her
              answerphone.

Tom brings the microphone centre stage.

              I think that ships well and truly sailed now.
              It's starting to sink in.
              I go out with my mate Charlie drinking
              I fill my boots, don't get me wrong, but at
              the end of the night.
              Whatever girl I'm with, there's only one
              that's on my mind.

As I stand at Vauxhall bus stop, on a massive comedown,
Contemplating everything that went wrong
Thinking, if only I had my guitar with me now I could write her a song...

TOM clocks his guitar. Winks. Picks it up.

And as I await the 108 home.
As the rain hit's my face, I'm staring at my phone.

Tom plays...

Grey With the Duffer On

And it's fireworks as her name flashes.
Wait before I answer
Like I wasn't just sat waiting for her name to flash
before I answered.
Give it a four second pause...

"Tom, is there a reason you've left me forty-seven
missed calls?"

"Yeah I was just calling to see if I left that grey duffer
top at yours?
You know the grey one that's got 'Duffer' written on it.
That's grey?"

"You know the grey one the Duffer one that one I know
full well is there. And even if you've thrown it away I
wunt care. But any excuse ey?"

"It's here" she says "I can meet you with it."

"So you'll come meet me with it

But you won't come without it?
And then I'll be here with it,
But not really with it
Knowing that I'm without you,
Unless you'll come without it
And complete me?
I mean, complete the... outfit.
Which is why I called again and again
Cuz I can't find the matching joggers either.
And I start football training on Tuesday and I really
need 'em

Y'know the grey ones.
The grey ones with, 'Duffer' not 'Duffle' on.
Yeah those ones with ruffle on the badge,
You know that badge that used to drive you mad when it
rubbed across... You've not see 'em?
No worries I'll have another look alright, take care
then...speak soon"

"Look I know we haven't spoke in a while now and it's
getting pretty late, But I've just been out right and I
swear I just bumped into your mate.
What's his name? Blake. Or Blaine?
I don't know all your mates sound the same.

Y'know the gay one. The gay one, with all the muscle on
him?
Yeah, y'know the grey one with the Duffer on it?
And I haven't slept since you left and I've must have
wrote you a thousand texts I haven't sent, just sat on our
bench.

You know the grey one. The grey on with all the rubble
on it?
Engrained with our names on, we used to cuddle on it.
And jump into puddles from it.

And that time when that lad caught us shagging
And we thought we'd got into trouble for it?"

Well I've slept on that bench, until I'm drenched.
And in my dreams...

You drive past and see me in lying on those slabs
In Forest Hill round the back of my old flat
The proper grey one's, the grey one's and I suffer on it,
My top's soaking wet. The rain comes and I blubber on it.
The pain comes and I shudder on it.

And in my dreams you pick me up.

And that's when I ask. "Why'd you never call me back?"

And you say. "Because I didn't know what to say Tom."

"Just say you've still got that Duffer top of mine."

"You mean... The grey one?"

END.